MARILYN
FOR BEGINNERS

MARILYN
FOR BEGINNERS™

KATHRYN HYATT

Writers and Readers Ltd.
35 Britannia Row
Islington
London N1 8QH
e-mail: begin@writersandreaders.com
web address: writersandreaders.com

Published by Writers and Readers by arrangement with Seven Stories Press, New York USA.

Text and Illustration Copyright Kathryn Hyatt: © 1998
Cover Illustration: Kathryn Hyatt
Cover Design: Paul Gordon

This book is sold subject to the conditions that it shall not, by way of trade or otherwise, be lent, re-sold, hired out, or otherwise circulated without the publisher's prior consent in any form of binding or cover other than that in which it is published and without a similar condition being imposed on the subsequent purchaser.

All rights reserved. No part of this publication may be reproduced, stored in a retrieval system, or transmitted in any form or by any means, electronic, mechanical, photocopying, recording, or otherwise, without prior permission of the publisher.

A CIP catalogue record for this book is available from the British Library.

A Writers and Readers For Beginners™ Documentary Comic Book.
Copyright © 1998
ISBN 0-86316-269-X

1 2 3 4 5 6 7 8 9 0

Manufactured in the E.U.

For Beginners™ Comic Books are published by Writers and Readers Ltd. Its trademark, consisting of the words "For Beginners, Writers and Readers Documentary Comic Books" and Writers and Readers logo is registered in the U.S. Patent and Trademark office and in other countries.

dedication

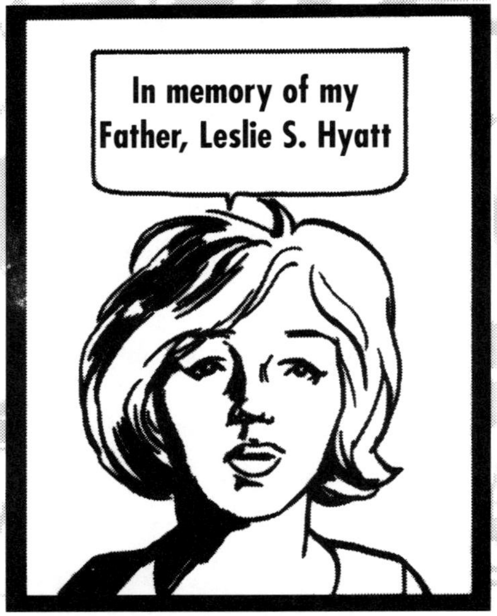
In memory of my Father, Leslie S. Hyatt

about the author

Kathryn Hyatt's graphic stories have appeared in World War 3 Illustrated and Girl Talk. Her interest in Marilyn Monroe began when she was nine years old and saw *Gentlemen Prefer Blondes*.

table of

contents

Chapter one 1
Mama's Girl

Chapter two 25
The Girl Least Likely to Succeed

Chapter three 62
The Man Who Knew Me Too Well

Chapter four 81
Up From Way Down

Chapter five 120
Back To Hollywood

Chapter six 138
The Lost Interview

Afterword 154

ABOUT THE BOOKS

Writers and Readers will be 25 in the year 2000. Our For Beginners Documentary Comic Books have grown with us to become internationally recognised and has even attracted imitators.

Writers and Readers For Beginners books are introductions to some of the major thinkers of our time. Their form pioneers an attempt to bring words and images together and to translate the most complicated information into a simple, readable and amusing story.

Originally intended for the uninitiated, experts from all over the world have come to admire and use the series. We began the series with books on Cuba For Beginners (1975) by Mexican Cartoonist Rius, followed by Marx For Beginners (1976) also by Rius. These provided stepping stones for future books in history, philosophy, linguistics, psychiatry, black studies, literature, religion, biology, theatre and the media. New lines of development are continuing.

While the For Beginners series was originally published in England, it is today available in 16 languages and in many of the world's major cities, from Toyko to New York.

Free catalogue on request from :

Writers and Readers Ltd.
35 Brittania Row
London N1 8QH
Tel: 0171 226 3377
Fax: 0171 833 4804
email: begin@writersandreaders.com
web address:writersandreaders.com

I LEARNED THAT WHEN I WAS VERY BAD, I GOT THE RAZOR STROP.

WHEN I WAS A LITTLE BAD, I GOT ATTENTION.

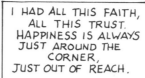

It was really the English family that introduced me to the movies. On Saturdays they'd take me to Grauman's Chinese or Egyptian.

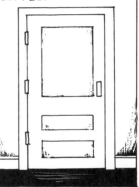

BY THE TIME I WAS TWENTY I HAD FOUND SOME SUCCESS WORKING AS A MODEL AND PIN-UP GIRL, ENOUGH SUCCESS TO BE NOTICED BY A MOVIE STUDIO.

I SIGNED A CONTRACT WITH TWENTIETH CENTURY FOX. A YEAR LATER — WITH A NEW NAME AND ONE PERFORMANCE ON THE CUTTING ROOM FLOOR I WAS DISMISSED FOR BEING "UNPHOTOGENIC."

IN A TOWN FULL OF BEAUTIFUL STARLETS ASPIRING TO BE THE NEXT BETTY GRABLE OR RITA HAYWORTH, I WAS ——

The Girl Least Likely to Succeed ②

1948 — MARCH — 1948

THE ACTOR'S LAB

"HAIL TO THEE BLITHE SPIRIT, SWEET BIRD THAT THY WIRTH..."

VERY GOOD, EXCELLENT PROJECTION, ... NOW MISS MONROE.

GULP

HAIL TO THEE BLITHE SQUEAK

*DARYL ZANUCK, STUDIO HEAD AND CO-FOUNDER OF TWENTIETH CENTURY FOX.

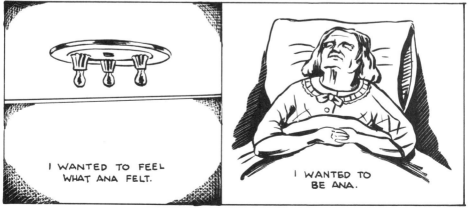

IN SPITE OF EVERYTHING I WENT TO MY ACTING CLASS NEXT DAY. I HAD WORKED SO HARD TO GET THIS FAR, EVEN THOUGH IT WASN'T VERY FAR AT ALL.

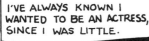

I WAS WORKING HARD, LEARNING MY TWO SONGS, PRACTICING MY DANCE ROUTINES...

AND STUDYING MY LINES.

MAMA, HE'S NOT LIKE DADDY. HE'S DIFFERENT.

GOOD, MUCH BETTER.

I ADMIT I DIDN'T SEE MUCH POTENTIAL IN YOU, BUT YOU'RE REALLY IMPROVING.

THANK-YOU, NATASHA.

THAT MEANS A LOT COMING FROM YOU, YOU'RE SUCH A CULTURED WOMAN.

THERE IS SO MUCH I WANT TO LEARN.

DID YOU READ THE BOOK I LENT TO YOU?

YES. CHEKHOV REALLY UNDERSTOOD PEOPLE, DIDN'T HE?

HE WAS A PERSON OF GREAT HUMANITY.

CHEKHOV EMBODIES THE RUSSIAN SOUL!

CHEKHOV IS ONE OF THE GREAT MODERN DRAMATISTS.

MY RELATIONSHIP WITH MISS NATASHA LYTESS HAD GREATLY IMPROVED.

WHEN THE TIME CAME TO FILM **LADIES OF THE CHORUS** I ARRIVED EARLY AT THE SOUNDSTAGE EACH DAY.

STILLS FROM **LADIES OF THE CHORUS**

I HAD REHEARSED AND MEMORIZED MY LINES WORD PERFECT.

IT WAS ONLY A "B" MOVIE, BUT YOU NEVER KNOW.

YOU HAVE TO TREAT EVERYTHING SERIOUSLY, AS IF THIS WERE YOUR BIG BREAK.

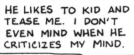

JOHNNY LEFT HIS WIFE AND TWO SONS. HE BOUGHT A HOUSE IN BEVERLY HILLS AND I MOVED IN WITH HIM. IN THE DINING ROOM JOHNNY INSTALLED FOUR WHITE LEATHER BOOTHS AND A DANCE FLOOR. IT WAS OUR OWN PRIVATE ROMANOFF'S.

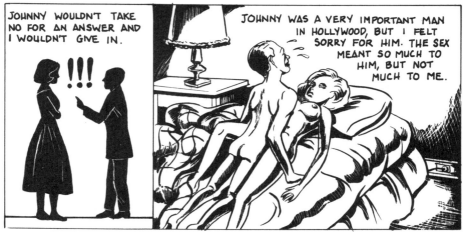

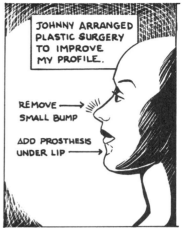

FIVE MONTHS INTO MY NEW CONTRACT AT FOX. I'M CAST IN TWO MOVIES SO BAD THEY NEED A BLONDE (ME) TO KEEP THE AUDIENCE AWAKE.

MY PARTS ARE NEVER IMPORTANT, BUT I'M ALWAYS ON THE POSTER. IT'S GETTING HARDER TO BELIEVE I'M PAYING MY DUES, THAT THIS IS LEADING SOMEWHERE.

STILL, I CONTINUE TO STUDY ACTING WITH MICHAEL CHEKHOV.

THE ORCHARD IS ALL WHITE. YOU'VE NOT FORGOTTEN IT? LUBA?

A SCENE FROM *THE CHERRY ORCHARD*.

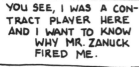

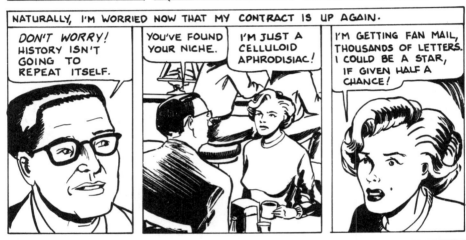

THAT NIGHT I LEFT WITH MR. SKOURAS. NEXT MORNING HE ORDERED THE STUDIO TO FEATURE ME IN AS MANY FILMS AS POSSIBLE.

MY CONTRACT IS SECURED FOR ANOTHER SEVEN YEARS.

NIAGARA 1953

THE LAST ROADBLOCK TO STARDOM, IF NOT ACTING, HAD BEEN REMOVED.

THERE'S NO BUSINESS LIKE SHOW BUSINESS 1954

MY LIFE WOULD BE CHANGED FOREVER.

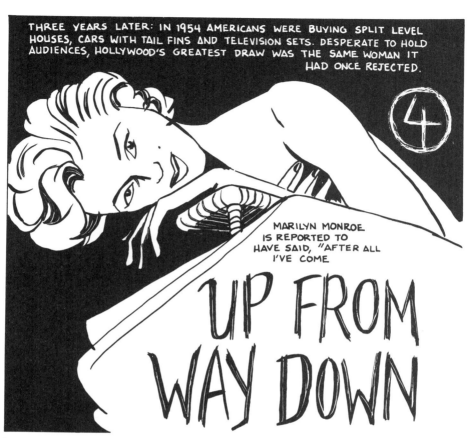

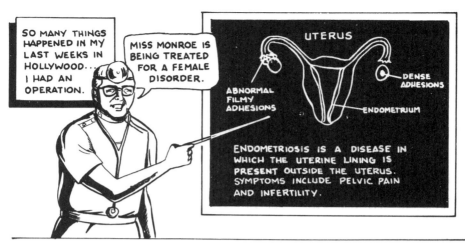

Miss Fitzgerald's performances sold out every night. Soon, other Negro entertainers followed.

If only I could solve my own problems so easily.

MY LAST DAYS IN HOLLYWOOD WERE SO BUSY.

I POSED FOR PUBLICITY PICTURES FOR *THE SEVEN YEAR ITCH*.

I MET THE ENGLISH POET, EDITH SITWELL...

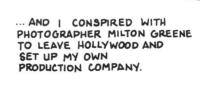

... AND I CONSPIRED WITH PHOTOGRAPHER MILTON GREENE TO LEAVE HOLLYWOOD AND SET UP MY OWN PRODUCTION COMPANY.

I GAVE UP THE LEASE OF MY HOUSE AND MOVED IN WITH MY OLD FRIEND AND FRED'S SISTER, MARY KARGER.

I HAD GONE UNDERGROUND.

Everyone wants Marilyn, though. Connecticut is the last place anyone would expect to find me.

Imagine Lorelei Lee at the hardware store,

Pola at the A&P.

At night I read in my room. I've read about Josephine Bonaparte. Now I am reading about Isadora Duncan

...hardware... a at the A&P. At night I read in m... room. I've read about Josephine Bonaparte. Now I'm reading about Isadora...can.

These women inspire me because they turned their lives around, as I hope to do.

I am trying to build a good opinion of myself. Your kindness means everything to me.

I hope we will meet again soon. I kept all your letters. I often think of you.

SHOULD I SAY THAT? HE'S A DECENT MAN. HE'S STILL MARRIED.

PERHAPS I'M BEING TOO PUSHY.

BUT WHEN WILL I SEE HIM AGAIN?

I HAVE TO SEE HIM AGAIN. I JUST HAVE TO.

WITH SUCCESS COMES PROBLEMS. I WAS USED TO CRITICISM, BUT NOT THE SORT MY ROMANCE WITH ARTHUR DREW.

THE PRESIDENT OF 20TH CENTURY FOX, SPYROS SKOURAS, PAID ARTHUR AND ME A PERSONAL VISIT AT MY APARTMENT.

ARE YOU IN LOVE, SWEETHEART?
YES.

WONDERFUL! YOU'RE A LUCKY MAN, ARTHUR. TAKE GOOD CARE OF HER, SHE'S LIKE A DAUGHTER TO ME!

I HOPE YOU'RE NOT GOING TO MAKE A MISTAKE WITH THE COMMITTEE.

I CAN ONLY DO WHAT'S RIGHT.
I KNOW THESE MEN.

THEY CAN BE REASONABLE. A PRIVATE SESSION CAN BE ARRANGED. YOU UNDERSTAND?

MR. SKOURAS, I CANNOT CO-OPERATE WITH THE COMMITTEE.

ARTHUR YOU HAVE MORE THAN YOURSELF TO THINK OF NOW. WHAT COULD THIS DO TO MARILYN'S CAREER?

I'VE TOLD ARTHUR NOT TO WORRY ABOUT ME. I WILL SUPPORT HIM WHATEVER HE DECIDES TO DO.

PEOPLE IN HOLLYWOOD ARE SUCH COWARDS.

*WALTER WAS CHAIRMAN OF HUAC.

BACK TO HOLLYWOOD

MY CHARACTER, SUGAR KANE, IS A SINGER AND UKELELE PLAYER IN AN ALL GIRL BAND.

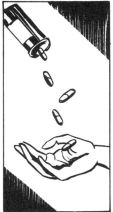

AT OTHER TIMES, I COULDN'T IGNORE THE HOSTILITY.

I USED TO LOVE TO PLAY WHEN I WAS LITTLE. THEN I LEARNED THIS WAS "ACTING". I LIKE THE CREATIVE PART OF ACTING.

ON THE SET OF *SOMETHING'S GOT TO GIVE* WITH DIRECTOR GEORGE CUKOR.

MARILYN, MEET YOUR "CHILDREN," CHRIS AND ALEXANDRA.

WE'RE GOING TO HAVE A LOT OF FUN ON THIS FILM, I PROMISE.

ONLY THINGS GET BETWEEN YOU AND ACTING. SOMETIMES YOU SEE HUMAN NATURE AT ITS VERY WORST.

IF MY BABY HAD LIVED, SHE WOULD HAVE BEEN THE SAME AGE AS THAT LITTLE GIRL.

WHY WOULD THEY CAST THAT WOMAN AS A MOTHER?

IF THEY SEE YOU'RE VULNERABLE, THEN THEY GO IN FOR THE KILL.

EVERYONE KNOWS SHE'S THE BIGGEST WHORE IN THE WORLD.

IN THIS SCENE, YOU SEE YOUR CHILDREN FOR THE FIRST TIME IN FIVE YEARS.

PLACES.

IN THE EDITOR'S OFFICE OF A POPULAR WOMAN'S MAGAZINE.

AFTERWORD

I was standing in my kitchen making toast and thinking about shopping for school clothes, when the news of Marilyn Monroe's suicide came over the radio. That moment, exactly where I stood, the August morning light, are fixed in my memory like a polaroid shot. I was shocked. How could anyone so alive be dead? It hardly mattered that I had never met the woman. By the time I was twelve, Marilyn Monroe already had a grip on my imagination.

As I was growing up, I would rediscover Marilyn Monroe every few years. I eagerly consumed each revived film, discovered photograph, and new book. Marilyn seemed to grow in depth and complexity as I did. When I became an artist, a woman artist at that, my empathy for Marilyn grew. I became dissatisfied with the way she was portrayed in the media. The glitzy, artificial icon, the simpering self-destructing addict, the sexual adventuress, the victim of a dozen different conspiracy theories—all distort, oversimplify, and deprive her of her humanity. "My" Marilyn was flawed, funny, brave, troubled, but, most of all, hard to pin down. I appreciate that about Marilyn. She frustrates all attempts to have the final say, to own her. In life Marilyn fought all attempts to categorize her, to limit her. She still insists on being her own person.

This is a fictionalized biography of Marilyn Monroe, based on my research and imagination. My methods are not unlike film biographies, which use composite characters, condensation of time, and *educated guesses.* In Chapter One, I imagine Marilyn telling the story of her childhood in a psychiatric session. It is true that Marilyn Monroe was a patient of psychiatrist Dr. M. Kris, as are the facts of her childhood presented here, but what was actually said in those sessions is sealed. In Chapter Two, there is a scene where Marilyn visits a graveyard. A number of people have asked me if this is something I imagined. It is a story Marilyn told to her husband, Arthur Miller. He apparently believed it and published it in his autobiography. That's good enough for me. In Chapter Four, Marilyn meets with a studio executive and lays out her complaints about how her contract limited her choice of roles. This probably never occurred as a one-on-one meeting, but was carried out between lawyers over a period of months. For dramatic purposes and for the sake of readers' attention spans, the incident is reduced to a one-page confrontation. Chapter Six, "The Lost Interview," was based in part on an interview Marilyn gave to the French magazine MARIE CLAIRE and an interview and photo session she gave to LIFE magazine that was published a few days before her death. The woman interviewer was based on Flora Rheta Schreiber whose interview for GOOD HOUSEKEEPING magazine was killed for being too sympathetic. As for Marilyn's "voice," I built my dialogue from existing interviews and my own sense of how Marilyn would speak.

Researching this book, I read everything that I could find currently in print on Marilyn Monroe. Some of my primary sources were LEGEND by Fred Lawrence Guiles, MY STORY by Marilyn Monroe, MARILYN MONROE by Donald Spoto, GODDESS by Anthony Summers, THE UNABRIDGED MARILYN: HER LIFE FROM A TO Z by Randall Riese and Neal Hitchens and Arthur Miller's autobiography, TIMEBENDS. There are a wealth of photo surveys devoted to Marilyn Monroe. Some of the ones I most relied on were MARILYN AMONG FRIENDS by Sam Shaw, MONROE by James Spada, and MARILYN AT TWENTIETH CENTURY FOX by Lawrence Crown. Many hours were spent at the New York Public Library, both at the picture collection and the Billy Rose collection, which supplied photo material for my drawings of automobiles, movie houses, street cars, fashions, the Empress Josephine, and more.

There are a number of people whose help I gratefully acknowledge: Suzanne Ball, Ann Decker, Howard Kogan, Peter Kuper, Seth Tobocman, and my editor and publisher, Dan Simon, who took a chance on me.

what's

FOR BEGINNERS™

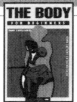

THE BODY FOR BEGINNERS ™
By Dani Cavallaro
Illustrated by Carline Vago
ISBN 0-86316-266-5
(UK £7.99)

What is the body? Is it a natural object? An idea? A word? **The Body For Beginners** ™ addresses these and other questions by examining different aspects of the body in a variety of cultural situations.

It argues that in recent years the body has been radically re-thought by both science and philosophy. Science has shown that it can be disassembled and restructured. Philosophy has challenged the traditional superiority of the mind over the body by stressing that corporeality is central to our experience and knowledge of the world.

Exploring the part played by the body in society, philosophy, the visual field and cyberculture and drawing examples from literature, cinema and popular culture, mythology and the visual arts, **The Body For Beginners** ™ suggests that there is no single way of defining the body. There are eating bodies, clothed bodies, sexual, erotic and pornographic bodies, medical bodies, technobodies, grotesque and hybrid bodies, tabooed, cannibalistic and vampiric bodies - to mention just a few of the aspects considered in this book.

Framing the body is a vital means of establishing structures of power, knowledge, meaning and desire. Yet, the body has a knack of breaking the frame. Its boundaries often turn out to be unstable. And this instability can be both scary and stimulating at the same time.

This book will appeal to you if you are curious about the body as something more exciting and multi-faceted than simply a lump of meat!

GESTALT FOR BEGINNERS ™
By Sergio Sinay
Illustrated by Pable Blasberg
Translated by Mariana Solanet
ISBN 0-86316-258-4
(UK £7.99)

Gestalt For Beginners™ details the birth of the therapy, investigates the complex life of its creator Fitz Peris and describes his revolutionary techniques such as the *Empty Chair*, the *Monodrama* and the *Dream Studie*s. The author also demonstrates why Gestalt therapy is an ideal approach to self-affirmation and personal growth.

SAI BABA FOR BEGINNERS ™
By Marcelo Berenstein
Illustrated by Miguel Angel Scenna
Translated by Mariana Solanet
ISBN 0-86316-257-6
(UK £7.99)

120 million devotees worldwide recognise Sathya Sai Baba as a modern Hindu *avatr (*a human incarnation of the divine) with the ability to be in various places simultaneously and with absolute knowledge.

Why does this man claim to be God? Who gave him that title? And what did he come here for? **Sai Baba For Beginners**™ details Sai Baba's life from his birth in 1926 to his studies, miracles, works, programme of education in human valor and his messages, up to the celebration of his recent 70th Birthday.

FANON FOR BEGINNERS ™
By Deborah Wyrick Ph.D
ISBN 0-86316-255-X
(UK £7.99)

Make me always a man who questions
       -F. Fanon

Philosopher, psychoanalyst, politician, prophet -- Frantz Fanon (1925-1961) is one of the most influential writers on race and revolution. This book provides a clear, detailed introduction to the life and work of the man Jean-Paul Sartre called the voice of the third world.

Fanon For Beginners ™ opens with a biography, following Fanon from his birthplace in Martinique, through combat in World War II and education in France, to his heroic involvement in the fights for Algerian independence and African decolonization. The main section of the book covers the three principal stages of Fanon's thought:

The Search for Black Identity, as presented in a *Black Skin, White Masks,* the stunning diagnoses of racism that Fanon wrote while studying medicine and psychoanalysis.

The Struggle Against Colonialism, as explained in *A Dying Colonialism* and *Towards the African Revolution*, essays Fanon produced when he was actively engaged in Algeria's war of independence.

The Process of Decolonization, as analyzed in *The Wretched of the Earth*, the book that extended insights gained in Algeria to Africa and the Third World

What's new?

Writers and Readers

BENJAMIN FOR BEGINNERS ™
By Lloyd Spencer
ISBN 0-86316-262-2
(U.K. £7.99)

Benjamin For Beginners ™ offers a clear accessible guide to one of the most intriguing and inspiring thinkers of the 20th century. Since his suicide in 1940, the ideas of Walter Benjamin have influenced contemporary writers like Jacques Derrida, Paul de Man, George Steiner, John Berger and Terry Eagleton. Today, Benjamin's essays are hotly debated by students of cultural and media studies, by philosophers and by literary critics.

Benjamin wrote brilliant commentaries on major figures of literary modernism including Baudelaire, Proust, Kafka, Brecht and the Surrealists. He wrote as a modernist and his preoccupation with questions of language and with literary and artistic form extended to his experimental ways of conceiving and presenting his own writings.

STRUCTURALISM & POSTSTRUCTURALISM FOR BEGINNERS ™
By Donald Palmer
ISBN 0-86316-193-6
(U.K. £7.99)

Poststructuralism is a loosely knit intellectual movement, comprised mainly of ex-structuralists, who have either become dissatisfied with the theory or felt they could improve it.

The book's starting point is the linguistic theory of Ferdinand Saussure. It then moves on to the anthropologist Claude Levi-Strauss, semiologist and critic Roland Barthes, Marxist philosopher Louis Althusser, psychoanalyst Jacques Lacan and the deconstructionist Jacques Derrida.

The book concludes with the examination of the post-modern obsession with language and with radical claims of the disappearance of the individual -obsessions that unite the work of all these theorists.

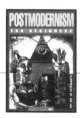

POSTMODERNISM FOR BEGINNERS ™
By Jim Powell
Illustrated by Joe Lee
ISBN 0-86316-188-X
(U.K. £7.99)

If you are like most people, you're not sure what Postmodernism is. And if this were like most books on the subject it probably wouldn't tell you.

Postmodernism For Beginners ™ features the thoughts of Foucault on power and knowledge, Jameson on mapping the postmodern, Baudrillard on the media, Harvey on time-space compression, Derrida on deconstruction, and Deleuze and Guattari on rhizomes. The book also discusses postmodern artifacts such as Madonna, cyberpunk, sci-fi, Buddhist ecology and teledildonics.

THE HISTORY OF CINEMA FOR BEGINNERS ™
By Jarek Jupść
ISBN 0-86316-275-4
(U.K. £9.99)

The History of Cinema for Beginners ™ is an informative introductory text on the history of narrative film and a reference guide for those who seek basic information on interesting movies. The book spans over one hundred years of film history, beginning with events leading up to the invention of the medium and chronicles the early struggle of the pioneers.

Readers are introduced to people behind and in front of the camera and presented with all major achievements of the silent and sound periods - even the most intangible film theories are explained and made easily digestible.

accept no substitute!

Great ideas and great thinkers can be thrilling. They can also be intimidating and complicated.

That's where **Writers and Readers For Beginners**™ books come in. **Writers and Readers** brought you the <u>very first</u> **For Beginners**™ book over twenty years ago. Since then, amidst a growing number of imitators, we've published some 70 titles (ranging from Architecture to Zen and Einstein to Elvis) in the internationally acclaimed **For Beginners**™ series. Every book in the series serves one purpose: to UNintimidate and UNcomplicate the works of the great thinkers. Knowledge is too important to be confined to the experts.

And Knowledge as you will discover in our Documentary Comic Books, is fun! Each book is painstakingly researched, humorously written and illustrated in whatever style best suits the subject at hand. That's where **Writers and Readers, For Beginners**™ books began! Remember if it doesn't say...

...it's not an original For Beginners book.

How to get great thinkers to come to your home...

For trade and credit card orders please contact our UK distributor:

Littlehampton Book Services Ltd.
10-14 Eldon Way
Littlehampton
West Sussex BN17 7HE

Phone Orders: 01903 828800
Fax Orders: 01903 828802
E-mail Orders: orders@lbsltd.co.uk
Accepted credit/debit cards: Access, Visa, Mastercard, American Express and Switch

Individual Orders:

Please fill out the coupon below
And send to:
Writers and Readers Ltd
35 Britannia Row
London N1 8QH

Catalogue:

Or contact us for a FREE CATALOGUE of all our **For Beginners**™ titles

- ADDICTION & RECOVERY (£7.99)
- ADLER (£7.99)
- AFRICAN HISTORY (£7.99)
- ARABS & ISRAEL (£7.99)
- ARCHITECTURE (£7.99)
- BABIES (£7.99)
- BENJAMIN (£7.99)
- BIOLOGY (£7.99)
- BLACK HISTORY (£7.99)
- BLACK HOLOCAUST (£7.99)
- BLACK PANTHERS (£7.99)
- BLACK WOMEN (£7.99)
- BODY (£7.99)
- BRECHT (£7.99)
- BUDDHA (£7.99)
- CHE (£7.99)
- CHOMSKY (£7.99)
- CLASSICAL MUSIC (£7.99)
- COMPUTERS (£7.99)
- THE HISTORY OF CINEMA (£9.99)
- DERRIDA (£7.99)
- DOMESTIC VIOLENCE (£7.99)
- THE HISTORY OF EASTERN EUROPE (£7.99)
- EROTICA (£7.99)
- FANON (£7.99)
- FOOD (£7.99)
- FOUCAULT (£7.99)
- GESTALT (£7.99)
- HEALTH CARE (£7.99)
- HEIDEGGER (£7.99)
- HEMINGWAY (£7.99)
- HISTORY OF CLOWNS (£7.99)
- I CHING (£7.99)
- ISLAM (£7.99)
- JAZZ (£7.99)
- JEWISH HOLOCAUST (£7.99)
- JUDAISM (£7.99)
- JUNG (£7.99)
- KIERKEGAARD (£7.99)
- LACAN (£7.99)
- MALCOLM X (£7.99)
- MAO (£7.99)
- MARILYN (£7.99)
- MARTIAL ARTS (£7.99)
- MCLUHAN (£7.99)
- MILES DAVIS (£7.99)
- NIETZSCHE (£7.99)
- OPERA (£7.99)
- PAN-AFRICANISM (£7.99)
- PHILOSOPHY (£7.99)
- PLATO (£7.99)
- POSTMODERNISM (£7.99)
- STRUCTURALISM & POSTSTRUCTURALISM (£7.99)
- PSYCHIATRY (£7.99)
- RAINFORESTS (£7.99)
- SAI BABA (£7.99)
- SARTRE (£7.99)
- SAUSSURE (£7.99)
- SEX (£7.99)
- SHAKESPEARE (£7.99)
- STANISLAVSKI (£7.99)
- UNICEF (£7.99)
- UNITED NATIONS (£7.99)
- US CONSTITUTION (£7.99)
- WORLD WAR II (£7.99)
- ZEN (£7.99)

Name: _____
Address: _____
_____
City: _____
_____**Post Code:** ___
Tel: _____
Credit/Debit Card: _____
Account Number _____
Expirary Date: _____

(orders by credit/debit cards should be directed to Littlehampton Book Services)

Individual Order Form
(clip out or copy complete page)

Book Title	Quantity	Amount
	Sub Total:	
	TOTAL:	